For Windows

super short cuts!

The fastest, easiest way to do it!

**Expanded edition teaches
essentials *plus* shortcuts!**

MICROREF®

Educational Systems, Inc.
Northbrook, IL 60062

Product Number S324

99 98 97   4 3 2 1

Printed in the United States of America

Welcome to Super Shortcuts! . . .

...the speediest guide to computer software. Our goal is to save you time. This guide provides the fastest, easiest ways to run your software program with the fewest number of keystrokes.

*This guide contains two parts. The first part is **Excel 97 Essentials at a Glance** where you can review basic software tasks, necessary concepts, and exciting new features. The second part presents a complete **Shortcut Reference** to the program.*

We encourage you to read the first part of this guide page by page. If you are an experienced user, you will gain a fresh perspective on the software with plenty of hidden shortcuts to speed your work. If you are new to this program, the first part of this guide will give you a well-rounded introduction and explain the basic concepts behind the commands.

*In addition, glance through the **Shortcut Reference** in the second part of this guide to discover hidden shortcuts not found on menus. You will find time-saving keyboard and mouse tricks that speed you through your work. Also scan the reference section for the most useful icons and learn how they work.*

*To further speed your work, use the comprehensive **Contents** and **Index** pages to look up quick alternatives to commands you use day in and day out. Finally, to review basic program concepts, study the **It Helps to Know** section at the end of this guide.*

Excel 97 Essentials at a Glance

Using Charts and Graphics

Programming

Shortcut Reference

EXCEL 97 ESSENTIALS AT A GLANCE

The **Excel 97 Essentials at a Glance** section of this guide is a learning tool.

Read through the following procedures for an introduction to basic Excel 97 tasks. This tour shows you how to create documents, edit data, format worksheets, insert charts and other graphics, and program your workbook.

These procedures provide a broad overview to Excel 97 that includes specific tasks, necessary concepts, and exciting new Excel 97 features. Whether you're seeking an overall understanding of the program, gaining insights, or learning about entirely new additions to the program, this section has something new for you.

OFFICE FEATURES

SHORTCUT BAR

The Shortcut Bar normally appears at the top of your screen. If you installed Office 97 using the Typical Installation option, this Shortcut Bar will appear only if you installed it in Office 95. If the Shortcut Bar does not appear, rerun Setup from the Office 97 CD to install it.

You can view the Shortcut Bar in a window and display different shortcuts at one time.

View shortcuts in a window . . . . `DRAG` background
When you move the Shortcut Bar off the top of your
screen, it appears in a resizable window. If you display
multiple Shortcut Bars (see below), they appear
clearly labeled in this window.

Resize shortcut window . . . . `DRAG` border
Drag the window's border to resize and reshape a
shortcut window.

View different shortcuts

1. `RCLICK` background
2. `CLICK` toolbar name

If there is no background space in the Shortcut Bar on
which to right-click, then right-click on the vertical
bar just before the first button. Shortcut bars include
Office, Desktop, QuickShell, Favorites, Programs, and
Accessories. If you select multiple Shortcut Bars, a
button representing each Shortcut Bar appears on the
current Shortcut Bar.

Get help

1. ▦ in title bar
2. **Contents and Index**

Add/remove buttons

1. ▦ in title bar
2. **Customize**
3. **Buttons** tab

You can add buttons to open workbooks that you use
frequently. Drag the workbook icon from the
Windows Explorer window to the Buttons tab.

Show/hide ToolTips

1. ▣ in title bar
2. **C**ustomize
3. **View** tab
4. **S**how ToolTips

Button size

1. ▣ in title bar
2. **C**ustomize
3. **View** tab
4. **L**arge buttons

Hide Shortcut Bar at Windows startup

1. ▣ in title bar
2. E**x**it
3. **No** button

This permanently removes the Shortcut Bar from automatically displaying. To display the Shortcut Bar, open "Program Files\Microsoft Office\Office\Microsoft Office Shortcut Bar."

Display Shortcut Bar at Windows startup. . . . . `DRAG ▢` icon

Use this procedure if you have previously followed the preceding procedure to hide the Shortcut Bar. Use Windows Explorer or My Computer to copy the "Program Files\Microsoft Office\Office\Microsoft Office Shortcut Bar" icon to the "\Windows\Start Menu\Programs\StartUp" folder.

OFFICE ASSISTANT

The Office Assistant starts automatically by default in your Office applications.

Get rid of the Assistant . . . .

Get the Assistant back again . . . .

Tell the Assistant when to pop up
automatically . . . . `RCLICK` title bar, **O**ptions
To turn off the Office Assistant, clear all options.

Open the Assistant or the Index when you
press F1

1. `RCLICK` title bar

2. **O**ptions

3. **R**espond to F**1** key

Use a different Office Assistant character

1. `RCLICK` title bar

2. **C**hoose Assistant

Open Help . . . . **H**elp, **C**ontents and **I**ndex
Access Help on the Excel menu bar. You may also set
F1 to open Help instead of the Office Assistant as
described above.

WEB TOOLBAR

Use the Web toolbar in your Office programs to browse your
company intranet or the Internet. You must be on a networked
intranet or have a modem and software to connect to the
Internet.

Show Web toolbar . . . .
Find this button on the Standard toolbar.

Hide all toolbars except Web toolbar . . . .
The Show Only Web Toolbar button is on the Web toolbar. Repeat to show the other toolbars that previously appeared.

Set the start page

1. Display start page

2. **Go ▾**

3. **Set Start Page**

Once you set the start page, you can connect to the Web and display the start page by clicking the Start Page button on the Web toolbar. You can also set the start page to any document on your disk to use the Web toolbar to open local documents.

Go to start page . . . .
The Start Page button is on the Web toolbar.

Set the search page

1. Display search page

2.

3. Set Search Page

Once you set the search page, you can connect to the Web and display the search page by clicking the Search the Web button on the Web toolbar. The search page might be a Web searcher page or a page with hyperlinks that provide easy access to other documents.

Go to search page . . . .
The Search the Web button is on the Web toolbar.

Go to any document or Web site . . . . type or select location in **Address** box

Cancel current action . . . . ⊗
Use the Stop Current Jump button on the Web toolbar whenever you want to stop the current action. Use it for example, when a Web page is taking too long to display.

START AND EXIT

Start Excel from the Windows Start menu

1. Ctrl Esc

2. <u>P</u>rograms

3. ⊠ Microsoft Excel

Start Excel and open a recently used workbook

1. Ctrl Esc

2. <u>D</u>ocuments

This menu lists recently used workbooks. Opening an
Excel workbook opens Excel and displays the
workbook.

Start Excel when you start Windows

1. Ctrl Esc

2. <u>S</u>ettings, <u>T</u>askbar

3. **Start Menu Programs** tab

4. <u>A</u>dd button

5. B<u>r</u>owse button

6. `2CLICK` Excel icon

Programs and documents in the StartUp folder start
automatically. To start Windows without starting
*these items, press **Shift** when the Windows logo*
appears during startup.

Open workbook(s) when you start
Excel . . . . move workbook icon to XLStart folder
Use Windows Explorer or My Computer to move
the icon or open the workbook and save it to the

XLStart folder. Find the XLStart folder in "Program Files\Microsoft Office\Office."

*Excel automatically opens all files in the Office\XLStart folder and the alternate startup folder. The alternate startup folder can be on a shared network drive. To set the alternate startup folder, select **Tools**, **Options**, **General** tab, **Alternate startup file location**.*

Change startup switches

1. **Ctrl Esc**
2. **Settings, Taskbar**
3. **Start Menu Programs** tab
4. **Advanced** button
5. **RCLICK** 🗶 Microsoft Excel
6. **Properties**
7. **Shortcut** tab
8. Type "**C:\...\EXCEL.EXE**" *switches*

*If you start Excel from the Office toolbar, right-click on the Excel button and select **Properties**.*

Examples:

C:\Microsoft Office\Excel\Excel.exe "C:\Data\Phone.xls"

Opens specific workbook.

C:\Microsoft Office\Excel\Excel.exe /r "C:\Data\Phone.xls"

Opens specific workbook as read-only.

C:\Microsoft Office\Excel\Excel.exe /e

Prevents startup screen and does not open a blank document.

C:\Microsoft Office\Excel\Excel.exe /p "C:\Data\"

Specifies the working folder.

C:\Microsoft Office\Excel\Excel.exe /e /p "C:\Data\"

Combine switches as desired.

Exit Excel . . . . **Alt F4**
*Excel prompts you to save changes to any unsaved
workbooks.*

CREATE A WORKBOOK

Create a blank workbook . . . . *or* **Ctrl N**
*A blank, default workbook also appears when you
start up Excel unless you have created a template
named "book" in Office\XLStart.*

Create default workbook template

   1. Ctrl N

   2. Edit and format workbook

   3. File, Save As

   4. Select **Template** file **type**

   5. At filename, type **book**

   6. Select **Office\XLStart** folder or alternate startup folder

   7. Save button

*A new workbook based on the default template will
appear whenever you start up Excel, select the New
tool, or press **Ctrl N**.*

Create a workbook based on

a template. . . . . **File, New**
*You will find Excel templates in the **Spreadsheet
Solutions** or other custom tabs. The Village Software*

---

template tells you how to order more templates.
Double-click the template to use. You may find
additional templates not installed with Typical
Installation on the Office 97 CD (add them to your
computer by running Setup on the CD).

Create a template

1. **Ctrl N**
2. Edit and format the workbook
3. **File, Save As**
4. Select **Template** file **type**

Save the template in the Microsoft Excel\Templates
or Office\Templates folder or subfolders of the
Templates folder.

Modify a template

1. **Ctrl O**
2. Edit and format the template
3. **Ctrl S**

The modifications only affect new workbooks created
with the template, not existing workbooks based on
the template.

To modify a built-in template in the
Templates\Spreadsheet Solutions folder, make
changes to the Customize sheet only.

Create a Web page . . . . **File, Save As HTML**

First, create a new document and add hyperlinks as
*desired (see **Insert a Hyperlink** section).*

This command starts the Internet Assistant add-in to
convert the workbook to a Web page.

Create a form

Web page . . . . <u>T</u>ools, <u>W</u>izard, <u>W</u>eb Form

First, create a form, including ActiveX controls for user navigation (see Insert a Control section).

This command starts Webform Wizard to set up a form that supplies data to a database. The Wizard helps you set up the elements of the form as a Web page.

You must have installed Wizards when you installed Excel.

OPEN AND CLOSE A WORKBOOK

Open a workbook . . . . Ctrl O

Open a recently used

workbook . . . . <u>F</u>ile, number

A list of the workbooks you last used appears on the bottom of the File menu. To set the number of documents that appear in the File menu, select Tools, Options, General tab, and type the number of desired Recently used file list entries.

Recently used file list

Hide workbook . . . . <u>W</u>indow, <u>H</u>ide

Workbook remains open but hidden.

Unhide workbook . . . . <u>W</u>indow, <u>U</u>nhide

Save workbook . . . . Ctrl S

Close a workbook . . . . Ctrl F4

Excel prompts you to save changes.

Set default folder

1. Tools, Options
2. General tab
3. Default file location

The file location is the pathname of the folder that Excel will display when you press Ctrl O to open a workbook. This is also the folder that Excel will suggest when you save a new workbook.

WORK WITH WORKSHEETS

Go to sheet .... `CLICK` `\Sheet/`
Click a sheet tab at the bottom of the window.

Rename sheet .... `2CLICK` `\Sheet/`
The name of the sheet appears on the sheet tab.

Insert new sheet (before current) .... Shift F11

**Delete current or selected
sheets** .... Edit, Delete Sheet

Set number of worksheets in new workbooks

1. Tools, Options
2. General tab
3. Sheets in new workbook

The default number of worksheets is 3.

Move sheet .... `DRAG` `\Sheet/`

Copy sheet. .... Ctrl `DRAG` `\Sheet/`

Hide sheet. .... Format, Sheet, Hide

Unhide. .... Format, Sheet, Unhide

PRINT, FAX, E-MAIL, AND ROUTE

Set print area. . . . . **File, Print Area**
*First, select cells or sheets to print. Set the print area
when you only print certain cells or sheets.*

Paper and layout settings . . . . **File, Page Setup**
*If a Chart is selected, the Page Setup dialog box
includes a Chart tab for setting up charts to print.
Otherwise, it includes a Sheet tab.*

Print preview . . . . 🔍

Exit preview . . . . **Esc**

Print and set print options . . . . **Ctrl P**
Displays the Print dialog box.

Print using current print options . . . . 🖨
*First, place pointer over Print tool to display a
ToolTip showing the default printer. This tool sends
output to the printer without displaying the Print
dialog box. It uses existing Print dialog box settings.*

Fax workbook
1. **File, Print**
2. Select fax driver at **Name**
*You must have fax software installed such as
Microsoft Fax.*

E-mail workbook . . . . **File, Send To, Mail Recipient**

Route workbook . . . . **File, Send To, Routing Recipient**

SHARE WORKBOOKS

You can allow multiple users to edit the same workbook at the same time. The result is one file with multiple changes, each marked as having been made by a specific user. You can later accept or reject individual changes made by other users.

Excel also allows you to distribute multiple copies of the workbook and then incorporate all the changes by "merging" the changed workbooks with your original workbook.

Edit workbook at the same time as other users

1. **Tools, Share Workbook**
2. **Editing** tab
3. **Allow changes**

This procedure enables multi-user change tracking whereby Excel highlights changes made by each user and provides a descriptive comment of each change. You can later review and accept or reject changes made by other users.

To let other users access the workbook, be sure to save it on a network drive. When other users are working in the shared workbook at the same time, this dialog box displays user names.

Distribute copies of the workbook and track changes

1. <u>T</u>ools
2. <u>T</u>rack Changes
3. <u>H</u>ighlight changes
4. <u>T</u>rack changes

First, follow this procedure with the workbook displayed, then save the workbook and distribute it to other users. Give each copy a different name.

You can have Excel highlight changes on the screen and/or create a History sheet at the end of the workbook that lists changes. If you have Excel highlight changes on the screen, changed cells are marked in the upper-left corner. If you position the pointer over a changed cell, a comment appears that describes the change.

Excel does not track all changes made. For example, Excel does not track formatting changes, cell comments, and changed formula results due to a change to data in a cell referred to by the formula.

Accept or reject revisions

1. **T**ools
2. **T**rack Changes
3. **A**ccept or Reject

If you followed either of the above two procedures and reviewers have entered their changes, you can open the shared workbook or open each copy of a distributed workbook and review (accept or reject) reviewers' changes. If you distributed the workbook, use the next procedure to merge the changes that you accepted in individual copies into your original workbook.

Merge changes into current workbook

1. **T**ools
2. Merge **W**orkbooks

First, open the original workbook into which changes will be added from distributed copies. Use this procedure after you have reviewed and accepted or rejected changes to copies of the workbook.

*You must merge workbooks before the change history date expires (**Tools, S**hare **Workbook, Advanced** tab). Do not remove the shared workbook status of workbooks before you merge. Doing so deletes the change history.*

Reviewers cannot use versions previous to Excel 97.

EDITING FEATURES

MOVE IN A WORKBOOK

Go to cell or named range	F5
Cell A1	Ctrl Home
Lower right corner of sheet	Ctrl End
Previous sheet	Ctrl PgUp
Next sheet	Ctrl PgDn
Any sheet	CLICK \Sheet/
Next pane	F6
Next open workbook	Ctrl Tab

USE INTELLIMOUSE

Microsoft IntelliMouse is a pointing device designed to help you scroll and zoom with fewer arm movements than a normal mouse. It has a wheel between the left and right mouse buttons. Make sure that you install the IntelliMouse using its setup program, which is separate from Office 97 installation.

Scroll up or down .... Rotate mouse wheel

Pan up or down .... Hold down wheel, move mouse
To speed up panning, move the mouse further from the origin mark in the vertical scroll bar.

Scroll automatically .... Click wheel, move mouse
To speed up scrolling, move the mouse further from the origin mark in the vertical scroll bar.

Cancel automatic scrolling . . . . `CLICK` _or any key_

Move cursor . . . . `CLICK`
Note that scrolling does not select a new active cell.
You must click where you wish to begin typing. On a
large worksheet, you may first want to zoom out,
click on a cell, and then zoom in.

Zoom in or out . . . . Ctrl Rotate mouse wheel

Show or hide detail
in an outline . . . . Shift Rotate mouse wheel
First, select a cell that summarizes data.

Have mouse zoom by default (rather than scroll)
1. Tools, Options
2. General tab
3. Check Zoom on roll with IntelliMouse

Change IntelliMouse options
1. Ctrl Esc
2. Programs
3. Microsoft Input Devices, Mouse

EDIT ROWS AND COLUMNS

Insert a row or column. . . . . Ctrl Shift +

Delete selected row/column . . . . Ctrl -

Set default column
width . . . . Format, Column, Standard Width
Sets the default column width for columns in the
current workbook.

Change column width . . . . `DRAG` column border

*Drag the border to the right of the column letter. As
you drag, Excel displays the column width
measurement.*

Fit column to widest cell . . . . `2CLICK` column border

Type a column width
1. `RCLICK` column letter
2. <u>C</u>olumn Width

Change row height . . . . `DRAG` row border

*Drag the border below the row number. As you drag,
Excel displays the row height measurement.*

Fit row to tallest cell . . . . `2CLICK` row border

Type a row height
1. `RCLICK` row number
2. <u>R</u>ow Height

SELECT CELL DATA

Select cell range . . . . `DRAG`

Select multiple cell ranges . . . . Ctrl `DRAG`

Row . . . . `CLICK` row number

Column . . . . `CLICK` column letter

**Select all cells in named
range** . . . . `CLICK` name in **Name** box

*The Name box is to the left of the formula bar and
lists named ranges in the workbook.*

3D range
1. Ctrl `CLICK` \Sheet/

---

2. Select cells on one sheet

A 3D range is the same range of cells selected on multiple sheets.

Move between selected ranges . . . . Tab/Shift Tab

Deselect . . . . Esc

SELECT ENTIRE SHEETS

Selecting a sheet does not select all cells in that sheet. Selecting multiple sheets allows you to format several sheets at once or to select a 3D range (see above).

Select sheet . . . . `CLICK` \Sheet/

Select multiple sheets . . . . Ctrl `CLICK` \Sheet/

Repeat to deselect a sheet.

Select all sheets
  1. `RCLICK` \Sheet/
  2. <u>S</u>elect all sheets

Deselect sheets
  1. `RCLICK` \Sheet/
  2. <u>U</u>ngroup sheets

EDIT CELL DATA

Set edit options
  1. <u>T</u>ools, <u>O</u>ptions
  2. **Edit** tab

*Turn off drag-and-drop editing, set the direction to move when you press **Enter** after editing a cell, and other settings.*

Delete contents of cell . . . . Backspace

Delete contents of selected cell(s) . . . . **Del**

Clear selected cell(s) . . . . **Edit, Clear**
*Clear formatting, cell data, comments, or all of the
above.*

Use a form to enter data

1. Type field names
2. Select field names and existing data
3. **Data, Form**
4. Select **OK** button

*In order to create a form, your worksheet must have
column labels that Excel can use as field names (e.g.,
Last Name, First Name, Address). To enter new data
or edit data, you must select the column labels and any
existing data below these labels.*

Next field in form . . . . **Tab**

Next record in form . . . . **Enter** *or* ↓

Previous record in form . . . . ↑

Finish form . . . . **Esc**

EDIT IN THE FORMULA BAR OR CELL

Edit mode . . . . **F2** *or* `2CLICK` cell
Edit cell data directly in cell.

Cancel cell edits . . . . **Esc** *or* ❌
The Cancel button is in the formula bar.

Save cell edits . . . . **Enter** *or* ☑
The Enter button is in the formula bar.

Get help entering formulas. . . . . ▣

The Edit Formula button is in the formula bar. The
Formula Palette shows a list of functions, the formula
result, and help entering function arguments.

Insert a function . . . . **Shift F3**

Enter a number as text . . . . **'number**

For example, type zip codes as text rather than as
values.

Insert range name **F3**

*To create a name, see **Name Cells** section below.*

Make reference absolute **F4**

This adds a $ before the column and row reference.
*Press **F4** repeatedly to make the reference relative or*
mixed. A column letter or row number preceded by a
$ does not change when the cell containing that
formula is copied.

Start a new line in cell . . . . **Ctrl Enter**

COPY AND MOVE

Copy to Clipboard . . . . ▣

*You can also press **Ctrl C** or **Ctrl Ins**.*

Move to Clipboard . . . . ▣

*You can also press **Ctrl X** or **Shift Del**.*

Paste contents of Clipboard . . . . ▣

*You can also press **Ctrl V** or **Shift Ins**.*

Paste values only

   1. Edit, Paste Special

   2. Values

*First, copy to Clipboard. Copies the results of
formulas rather than the formulas.*

Copy formula from cell above .... Ctrl '

Copy value from cell above................. Ctrl Shift "

**Copy current cell to selected cells
to right.**.................................... Ctrl R
*First, select cells in a row and include the cell
containing data to copy.*

Copy current cell to selected cells down .... Ctrl D
*First, select cells in a column and include the cell
containing data to copy.*

**Copy current cell to several
cells with mouse** .... Ctrl `DRAG` fill handle
                                        (bottom right +)

QUICK WAYS TO ENTER DATA

Sum cells .... Σ , `DRAG` cells to sum, **Enter**

View sum of selected cells .... *Status bar*
*When you select a range of cells, Excel automatically
adds them and shows the result in the Status bar at
the bottom of the window.*

Enter text by selecting from list................... Alt ↓
*Opens a list of other text entries in the current
column.*

Insert current date . . . . **Ctrl ;**

Insert current time . . . . **Ctrl Shift :**

Current date (updates) . . . . **=TODAY()**
Updates to the current date whenever Excel
recalculates the workbook.

Current date and time (updates) . . . . **=NOW()**
Updates to the current date and time whenever Excel
recalculates the workbook.

Enter linear series

1. Type initial values

2. Select initial values

3. **DRAG** fill handle (bottom right +)

Excel adds the step value to the first cell and
subsequent cells.

Example initial values:

1/1/97 2/1/97
5 10
1997 1998

No need to type more than the first value in series
such as:

9:00
Mon
Jan
Period 1
1st Qtr

To have Excel apply the initial values to the least
squares algorithm to generate the series, select the
initial values and cells to fill, then select **Edit, Fill,**
Series, Linear *and check* **Trend.**

Enter growth series

1. Type initial values
2. Select initial values and cells to fill
3. **E**dit, F**i**ll, **S**eries
4. Select **G**rowth type
5. Check **T**rend option

If the Trend option is unchecked, Excel multiples the first cell by the Step value. With the Trend option checked, Excel applies the initial values to an exponential curve algorithm ignoring the Step value.

Trend unchecked. Initial values: 1 4 5 Results: 1 2 4 8 16

Trend checked. Initial values: 1 4 5 Results: 1.21 2.71 6.06

NAME CELLS

Name cell(s) . . . . type name in *Name* box
*First, select cells to name. Find the **Name** box to the left of the formula bar. It lists names of all of the named ranges in the workbook. The name cannot contain spaces.*

Name from cell data . . . . Ctrl Shift F3
First, select label and data to name. Creates names from top row or left column of selection. For example, if you have field names at the top of the column, you can name the field data using the field name.

Name formula or value

1. **Ctrl F3**
2. Type name

---

3. Type formula/value in **Refers to**

Named formulas and values do not appear in a cell or in the Names box; however, you can use them in formulas. For example, set Discount to equal .9

Edit name . . . . **Ctrl F3**

Go to a named range . . . . `CLICK` name in **Name** box

Paste all names and their references
in worksheet . . . . **F3, Paste List**

First, select upper-left cell of blank area of worksheet. List will overwrite any existing data.

UNDO AND REPEAT

Undo last action . . . . **Ctrl Z**

Undo multiple actions. . . . .

Click the arrow to open a list of your last actions. Select the actions to undo. You must select an entire range of actions.

Repeat last action **F4**

Repeating actions can save you time. For example, if you are formatting cells, you can quickly apply the same format to more cells by repeating the last format.

FIND AND REPLACE

Find blank cells, formulas, etc. . . . . **F5, Special**

Finds particular types of data such as comments, cells dependent on the current cell formula, etc., that you specify.

Find data. . . . . **Ctrl F**
*To cancel a search, press **Esc**.*

Find next occurrence . . . . **Shift F4**

Find previous occurrence . . . . **Ctrl Shift F4**

Replace data . . . . **Ctrl H**

CALCULATE FORMULAS

Calculate manually or automatically
   1. <u>T</u>ools, <u>O</u>ptions
   2. Calculation tab
*By default, Excel calculates the worksheet whenever
you change data. If this slows down performance, you
can use manual calculation.*

Calculate current sheet manually . . . . **Shift F9**

Calculate all open workbooks . . . . **Ctrl =** *or* **F9**

INSERT COMMENTS

Attach notes to a cell to enter your comments. Use to annotate your own worksheet or to add comments when reviewing a worksheet.

A cell containing a comment shows a red triangle in the upper-right corner.

Add a comment . . . . **Shift F2**
Type comments in balloon. You can drag a white handle to resize the balloon. Cells with comments have a mark in the upper-right corner.

View comment . . . . position pointer over cell

Edit comment . . . . **RCLICK** cell, **Edit Comment**

Delete comment . . . . **RCLICK** cell, **Delete Comment**

Show Reviewing toolbar

   1. **View, Toolbars**

   2. **Customize**

   3. **Toolbars** tab

The Reviewing toolbar contains buttons for displaying and editing comments as well as moving between comments.

When you display the Reviewing toolbar, Excel adds it to the list of toolbars in the View Toolbars list. You then do not have to use steps 2 and 3 above.

Show all comments . . . .
The Show All Comments button, on the Reviewing toolbar, keeps all comments open on the screen as you work. Click the button again to close all comments.

Go to next comment . . . .

Go to previous comment . . . .

Hide comments and/or indicators

  1. Tools, Options

  2. View tab

You can hide comments, indicators, or both. Indicators are the red triangles that mark cells containing comments. If you hide comments, they do not appear when you position the cell pointer over a cell containing a comment.

Print comments

  1. File, Page Setup

  2. Sheet tab

  3. Comments

FORMAT CELLS

Formatting changes a cell's appearance without changing its content.

Format selected cells . . . . **Ctrl 1**
You can select a numeric format, alignment, orientation, font, border, pattern, or protection. You can also change the font and font attributes of selected text within a cell.

Apply an AutoFormat . . . . **Format, AutoFormat**
First, select cell(s) to format or click on a cell within a range of non-blank cells to format. You can select from many pre-designed table formats.

Copy format of current cell

1. CLICK ▢ 🖌️

   Pointer changes to 🖌️ while Format Painter tool is active.

2. DRAG ▢ cells to format

Copy format several times

1. 2CLICK ▢ 🖌️

   Pointer changes to 🖌️ while Format Painter tool is active.

2. DRAG ▢ cells to format
3. Repeat Step 2 for other cells
4. CLICK ▢ 🖌️

Clear formatting . . . . **E**dit, Clea**r**, **F**ormats

Merge selected cells

1. Ctrl 1

2. **Alignment** tab

3. **M**erge cells

Repeat to split merged cells.

ALIGN TEXT

Align text

1. Ctrl 1

2. **Alignment** tab

Set the vertical and/or horizontal alignment.

Align left, center, right . . . . , ,

Center text across columns . . . .

First, select cells, one of which contains a title to center. This button merges the selected cells and centers the title.

Indent text. . . . .

Each time you click the Increase Indent button, Excel further indents the text.

Decrease or remove indent . . . .

Rotate text

1. Ctrl 1

2. **Alignment** tab

3. **Orientation** box

You can click on a forty-five degree angle or type the number of degrees to rotate the text.

Wrap long text within a cell

1. Ctrl 1
2. **Alignment** tab
3. Check **Wrap text**

Breaks a long line into shorter lines within the current column width. If you adjust the column width, the text will rewrap.

Shrink long text within a cell

1. Ctrl 1
2. **Alignment** tab
3. Check **Shrink to fit**

Displays a long line of text in a smaller font so that it fits within the current column. If you adjust the column, the text will shrink or grow larger.

FORMAT NUMBERS

Apply a number format

1. Ctrl 1
2. **Number** tab

Apply currency format . . . .

While typing in currency, type a decimal point for cents.

Hide a decimal place . . . .

Excel displays the number rounded to the current decimal place; however, it does not change the underlying number in the cell.

Display another decimal place. . . . .

Preset number of decimal places in selected cells

1. **Ctrl 1** *(one)*
2. **Number** tab
3. **Number** category
4. Set **Decimal** places

*When you press **Enter** after typing a number in a cell, Excel automatically displays the number of decimals that you specify. If you are typing in currency, for example, you will not need to type a decimal point.*

Preset number of decimal places for all future typing

1. **Tools, Options**
2. **Edit** tab
3. Check **Fixed decimal**

This command affects future typing in all workbooks.

USE FONTS

Change the typeface, type size, attributes, and color of text and numbers in selected cell(s) or selected text within a cell.

Set default font for new workbooks

1. **Tools, Options**
2. **General** tab
3. Set **Standard font** and **Size**

Set default font for current workbook

1. F<u>o</u>rmat, <u>S</u>tyle
2. **Normal** style
3. <u>M</u>odify button
4. Font tab

Change font. . . . . `Arial` ▼

Click the arrow and select from the list of available fonts.

Change font size. . . . . `10` ▼

Type a font size or click the arrow and select from the list.

Bold, italic, underline . . . . **B** , *I* , <u>U</u>

Font color . . . . **A** ▼

To apply the current color (the color of the bar in the icon), click the icon. Or, click the arrow and select a different color.

BORDERS AND SHADING

Border cells. . . . . ▢ ▼

To apply a border around selected cells, click the Borders button. To apply a specific type of border, click the arrow.

Shade or color cells . . . . ◇ ▼

To apply the default color, click the Fill Color button. To apply a different color, click the arrow.

Add a patterned background

1. **Ctrl 1** *(one)*
2. **Patterns** tab

CHANGE A VIEW

Set view options

1. **Tools, Options**
2. **View** tab

Set which bars appear, how comments display, how objects display, and which worksheet elements appear in a window.

Hide formulas

1. **Ctrl 1** *(one)*
2. **Protection** tab
3. Check **Hidden**

*First, select cells to affect. After the above procedure, you must protect the worksheet using **Tools, Protection, Protect Sheet**.*

Split window into two panes . . . . **DRAG** ▭

Find the split box at the top of the vertical scroll bar. When pointer changes to ↕ you can drag. If you want to split horizontally at the active cell, double-click the split box.

Split into four panes . . . . **Window, Split**

First, position cell selector where you want split to occur. You can drag the pane dividers to resize panes.

Remove split. . . . . **2CLICK** ▭ pane divider

---

View multiple sheets . . . . **Window, New Window**
Switch to the new window and display a different
sheet in it. You can drag windows on the screen and
minimize or resize them. You can display both
windows on the screen at the same time using the
Window, Arrange *command.*

Zoom in or out. . . . . **View, Zoom**

Quick zoom . . . . `100%` ▼
Click the arrow and select a zoom percentage.

Full screen view. **View, Full Screen**
Hides everything on the screen but the workbook. To
exit Full Screen view, press ***Esc.***

Set page breaks . . . . **View, Page Break Preview**
You can drag page breaks to position them. You can
continue editing the worksheet in this view. To exit,
select ***View, Normal.***

Print preview. . . . . 🔍
To exit print preview, press ***Esc.***

VIEW THE DRAWING TOOLBAR

Show/hide Drawing toolbar . . . .
Use this toolbar to create drawings (AutoShapes) and text boxes and to format objects on the worksheet such as charts.

CREATE CHARTS

*Create charts as embedded objects on the worksheet or in a Chart sheet. When you create or select a chart, the Chart toolbar appears and the **Chart** command appears on the menu.*

Create a chart using Chart Wizard . . . .
*First, select data to plot, including data labels if any. Follow instructions on screen. To create the chart in a Chart sheet, select **As new sheet** or to create as an embedded object, select **As object in** at Step 4 in Chart Wizard.*

Create a chart on a Chart sheet F11
First, select data to plot, including data labels if any. Creates a chart using the default chart type.

Change default chart type
1. CLICK ☐ any chart
2. **C**hart, Chart **T**ype
3. Select type
4. **Set as default chart** button
5. **Cancel** button

For step 1, click on a chart embedded in the worksheet or go to the Chart sheet.

Edit embedded chart. . . . . `CLICK`
*Use the Chart toolbar, Drawing toolbar, and **C**hart menu to customize the chart.*

Format chart object. . . . . `2CLICK` object
This opens a dialog box with formatting options.

Format entire chart . . . . `RCLICK` chart background
This opens a shortcut menu from which you can select various chart options.

Set default chart colors
   1. **T**ools, **O**ptions
   2. **Colors** tab

Set default chart options
   1. **T**ools, **O**ptions
   2. **Chart** tab

Create a text box
   1. ![text box icon]
   2. `DRAG` on chart or sheet.
   3. Type text.
Find the Text Box tool on the Drawing toolbar. Use a text box to position a block of text anywhere on a sheet or chart. When you create a chart, the Drawing toolbar appears at the bottom of the window.

Edit text in box . . . . `CLICK` text box

Format an object . . . . 2CLICK ☐ object
For example, double-click the border of a text box.
Opens a dialog box where you can set properties for
the object.

DRAW AUTOSHAPES

Excel includes the Drawing toolbar with tools for creating
shapes called AutoShapes. AutoShapes are boxes, circles,
arrows, squares, lines, and other shapes.

Show/hide Drawing toolbar . . . .
Find this button on the Standard toolbar.

Create AutoShape

1. AutoShapes ▼

2. Select tool

3. DRAG ☐ in sheet

To create a proportional object (such as a square or
*circle), hold down **Shift** as you drag.*

Add text to an AutoShape

1. ☐ RCLICK AutoShape

2. **Add Text**

To edit text, click text area or repeat above and
*select **Edit Text**.*

Format an AutoShape . . . . 2CLICK ☐ AutoShape
Set colors, borders, size, and more.

CREATE WORDART OBJECTS

Create WordArt pictures to use text as a graphic element. When you create or select a WordArt object, the WordArt toolbar appears.

Create object. . . . . **Insert, Picture, WordArt**

Or, find the Insert WordArt tool on the Drawing toolbar.

Rotate selected object

1.
2. **DRAG** handle on object

The Free Rotate tool is in the WordArt toolbar. Pointer changes to while rotating.

Format selected object . . . .

Edit WordArt text. . . . . **2CLICK** object

WORK WITH OBJECTS

Objects include pictures, graphics, charts, text boxes, and other items on a worksheet.

Select object . . . . **CLICK**

If you have trouble selecting an object, click in the Drawing toolbar and then click the object. White handles appear around a selected object and often a toolbar appears. For example, if you select a WordArt object, the WordArt toolbar appears.

Select several objects . . . . **Shift CLICK**

Go to next/previous object . . . . Tab/Shift Ta|

Position an object . . . . DRAG |

Resize and reshape object . . . . DRAG | handl◄

Resize object proportionally . . . . Shift DRAG | handl◄
Use to maintain proportion, for example, of a
circle or square.

Size to fit cells . . . . Alt DRAG | handl◄
Object snaps to cell grid.

Group selected objects . . . . |RCLICK object, **G**rouping
You can move, flip, rotate, resize, and scale grouped
objects collectively. You can also change the format
and other attributes of all objects at once. Also use
this command to ungroup and regroup.

Change stack order . . . . |RCLICK object, O**r**der
Move an object before or behind others to expose or
hide it.

VALIDATE DATA

Set up data validation to specify the kind of data that users can enter into particular cells. For example, you can specify that a certain block of cells can contain only dates within a particular range of dates.

There are two ways to respond to invalid data: 1) prevent the cell from accepting any invalid data by displaying an error message when the user attempts to enter invalid data, or 2) allow the invalid data to be entered and then check for invalid data in the worksheet.

Set validation for selected cells

1. <u>D</u>ata, Va<u>l</u>idation
2. **Settings** tab

Create a data entry prompt

1. <u>D</u>ata, Va<u>l</u>idation
2. **Input Message** tab

Use to identify to the user what data they should enter into a particular cell. As soon as the user selects the cell, the prompt appears.

Create an error prompt

1. <u>D</u>ata, Va<u>l</u>idation
2. **Error Alert** tab

*When a user tries to enter invalid data in a cell, this setting displays an error message. By default, this feature is on. To allow users to enter invalid data, but mark the cell as containing invalid data, deselect **<u>S</u>how error alert.***

Show Auditing toolbar

  1. <u>T</u>ools, A<u>u</u>diting

  2. <u>S</u>how Auditing Toolbar

This toolbar helps you identify invalid data (see below).

Check for invalid data . . . .
Find the Circle Invalid Data button on the Auditing toolbar. It marks all cells containing invalid data with a red circle.

Remove invalid data marks . . . .
Find the Clear Validation Circles button on the Auditing toolbar.

INSERT A HYPERLINK

A hyperlink is text or a graphic that is active. If you click on it, you jump to another location or document. This could be a document on your hard disk, your network server, your company's intranet, or the Internet's World Wide Web and File Transfer Protocol (FTP) sites.

A hyperlink can jump to a named location in the same or a different document. For example, it could jump to a bookmark in a Word document, a named range in an Excel workbook, a database object, or a slide number. A hyperlink can also pre-address e-mail and open the user's e-mail editor (if installed).

If a hyperlink is text, it can either appear onscreen as the pathname or address destination to jump to or some other text such as "click here."

Insert text hyperlink . . . . **Ctrl K** *or*
*If desired, first select cell containing text to become
the hyperlink's active area that users will click. If you
do not select a cell containing text, Excel will insert
the address of the destination. If you have not set a
hyperlink base (see below) or do not wish to use it,
clear the **Use relative path for hyperlink** check box.*

Insert graphic hyperlink

1. Select graphic

2. **Ctrl K** *or*

*First, insert a graphic created in another file or use
the Drawing or Picture toolbar to create the graphic
in Excel.*

Set hyperlink base

1. **File, Properties**

2. **Summary** tab

3. **Hyperlink base**

*The hyperlink base is the root path of hyperlink
addresses (such as a server name). It is added to the
pathname of hyperlinks that you create using a
relative path. This makes it easy to change hyperlink
addresses when you change a server or directory
name. You need only change the name in the
hyperlink base to change it for all hyperlinks in a
workbook. It also means that you do not have to type
the entire address each time you create a hyperlink
when the destination resides in the same location.*

---

*To use the hyperlink base address in the address of a particular hyperlink, select **Use relative path for hyperlink** when you create the hyperlink. If not selected, the hyperlink ignores the hyperlink base.*

Follow (activate) hyperlink . . . . `CLICK` hyperlink
This opens the hyperlink destination.

Return to the original document . . . . ⇦
Find the Back button on the Web toolbar.

Cancel a hyperlink jump . . . . 🗙
Find the Stop Current Jump button on the Web toolbar. Use this button when the destination takes too long to display.

Select cell without activating hyperlink . . . . ↑↓←→
Use the arrow keys to move the cell selector to the cell containing the hyperlink. To edit the text, press F2.

Select graphic without activating hyperlink . . . . Ctrl `CLICK`
Use this method to select a graphic in order to edit or format it without activating the hyperlink.

Edit hyperlink destination
1. `RCLICK` hyperlink
2. **H**yperlink
3. Edit **H**yperlink

Set default format of hyperlinks in current workbook
1. F**o**rmat, **S**tyle
2. Hyperlink (**S**tyle name)

---

3. Modify

Excel applies the Hyperlink style to all hyperlinks. By default, Excel formats hyperlinks as underlined blue text. Excel applies the FollowedHyperlink style to all hyperlinks that you have used to jump to the destination. Excel formats Followed hyperlinks in purple underlined text.

The Hyperlink style does not appear in the **Style name** *list until you have created a text hyperlink. The FollowedHyperlink style does not appear in the* **Style name** *list until you activate a hyperlink in the workbook.*

INSERT A CONTROL

Controls are option buttons, check boxes, buttons that you press to run a macro, and other tools that are useful in forms and Web pages.

Use the Forms toolbar or Control Toolbox to create controls. Use Forms toolbar buttons to create normal controls (such as controls that require the user to make a selection then places the selection in a worksheet cell).

Use Control Toolbox buttons to create ActiveX controls. Excel stores the code that runs when the user selects a control with the ActiveX control itself. This is useful for forms that you will place on the Internet. You can open the Code window directly from ActiveX controls that you create.

Show Forms toolbar . . . . `RCLICK` any toolbar
From the list of available toolbars, check **Forms.**

Insert Forms

control . . . . `CLICK` Forms tool, `DRAG`
*Click the tool on the Forms toolbar for the control that
you would like to create. Then drag on the worksheet.*

Set Forms control operation

1. `RCLICK` control

2. **Format Control**

*You can set how a control operates based on the type of
control. For example, set what appears in a drop-down
box. Most controls are linked to cells, providing cells
with user entry information or displaying data from cells.*

Assign a macro to a Forms control

1. `RCLICK` control

2. **Assign Macro**

*Choose a macro to run when a user selects the control.
Not all Forms controls need macros.*

Show Control Toolbox . . . . `RCLICK` any toolbar
From the list of available toolbars, check **Control
Toolbox**.

Insert ActiveX

control. . . . . `CLICK` Control tool, `DRAG`
*Click the tool on the Control Toolbox for the control
that you would like to create. Then drag on the
worksheet. You can then create the Microsoft Visual Basic
code that runs when a user activates the control.*

Set properties for an ActiveX control

1. `RCLICK` control

2. **Properties**

Create code for an ActiveX control

1. **RCLICK** control
2. **V**iew Code

Opens the Microsoft Visual Basic Editor where you can write or open Visual Basic procedures and macros. Excel stores the code for ActiveX controls with the control itself. To exit the Code window, press Alt Q.

AUDIT FORMULAS

Show Auditing toolbar

1. **T**ools, A**u**diting
2. **S**how Auditing Toolbar

Use buttons on the Auditing toolbar to trace dependent and precedent cells, values and formulas that are causing errors in the worksheet, and invalid data. For more information on invalid data, see the Validate Data section above.

Trace dependents of current cell . . . .
Arrows show formulas that refer to the current cell.

Trace precedents of current cell . . . .
Arrows show cells that provide data to the formula in the current cell.

Trace errors in current cell . . . .
Use when a cell contains an error message and you do not know why. Red arrows point to cells containing a formula that is causing the error. Blue arrows point to cells containing a value that is causing the error.

Remove all arrows ....
Removes all arrows showing dependents, precedents,
and errors.

RECORD A MACRO

You can either record keystrokes and store them in a macro
or you can write macro commands. Excel stores macros
created in Excel 97 in Visual Basic format; however, Excel 97
can create and read macros from earlier versions of Excel.

If you record a macro, Excel stores the results of the
keystrokes in a module attached to the workbook. You can
copy macros between workbooks.

You can assign macros to a control created by the Form
toolbar or write a Visual Basic ActiveX program for a control
created by the Control Toolbox. Excel stores ActiveX
programs with the control itself, so you can use them in
creating Web pages.

You can create a Visual Basic macro to retrieve data from
another source.

Show Visual Basic toolbar. .... `RCLICK` any toolbar
*From the list of available toolbars, check **Visual Basic**.*

Record keystrokes .... `[•]`
The Record Macro button is on the Visual Basic
toolbar. Type a name for the macro (first character
must be a letter, no spaces allowed). Specify where to
store the macro. Your Personal Macro Workbook is
available during all Excel sessions. It is a hidden
workbook that Excel creates automatically when you
exit Excel after having stored the first macro there.
Excel names it PERSONAL.XLS in the XLStart folder.

---

*To assign a **Ctrl** or **Ctrl Shift** shortcut key to the*
*macro, select the **Options** button.*

Stop recording. . . . .
The Stop Recording button is on the pop-up toolbar
that appears when you start recording.

Run, edit, or delete a macro . . . . Alt F8
You can run, edit, or delete macros from any open
workbook. Therefore, if you want the macro to run
while another workbook is current, open the
workbook that contains the macro, then switch back
*to the current workbook with **Ctrl F6** and run the*
macro.

Stop macro . . . . Esc

PROTECT A WORKBOOK

Protect a workbook from modification or damage, (inadvertent
or otherwise) by users. You can protect general workbook
structure and window settings as well as specific cells, objects,
and sheets.

To prevent a user from changing a cell or object, you must
protect the entire worksheet and lock the individual cell or
object.

All cells and objects are locked by default. This means that if
you apply worksheet protection, all the cells and objects are
locked from user modification.

To enable users to change selected data or objects, first unlock
them individually, then apply worksheet protection.

Unlock cells

1. Select cells for users to modify

2. Format, Cells

3. Protection tab

4. Clear **Locked** checkbox

*This allows users to enter data into certain cells in an otherwise protected worksheet (after following the **Protect Data** procedure below). You can select multiple, nonadjacent cells by holding down **Ctrl** while you click on them.*

Unlock objects

1. Select objects for users to modify

2. Format

3. Select type of object

4. Protection tab

5. Clear **Locked** checkbox

*This allows users to modify graphic objects such as AutoShapes, objects, text boxes, pictures, and WordArt in an otherwise protected worksheet (after following the **Protect Data** procedure below).*

Protect data

1. Select sheets to protect

2. Tools, Protection

3. Protect Sheet

*First, unlock cells or objects that you want to allow users to modify and hide selected formulas you do not want others to see (press **Ctrl 1** (one), **Protection** tab, and check **Hidden**). This procedure protects the worksheet's contents, objects, and/or scenarios. To prevent others* *from changing protection settings, type a password (case sensitive).*

Move to next unprotected cell . . . . **Tab**

Unprotect data

1. Select sheets to unprotect
2. Tools, Protection
3. Unprotect Sheet

Protect structure and windows

1. Tools, Protection
2. Protect Workbook

This protects the workbook's structure (users cannot move, hide, insert, or rename worksheets) and/or windows (size and position). To prevent others from changing protection settings, type a password (case sensitive).

Save workbook with a password

1. File, Save As
2. Options button

You can prevent users from opening and using data in a worksheet or from editing and saving a worksheet. You also have the option of displaying a read-only recommendation message when users open the workbook.

Passwords are case sensitive. Write down the password for future reference.

Shortcut Reference

This section of the guide is a reference tool.

Use the index and table of contents to find the exact shortcut
you need. Since this section is organized by major menu
choices, you will also find shortcuts organized in simple, easy-
to-grasp categories.

In addition to specific shortcut keys, procedures give you
relevant, related information. For example, you will learn
where the cursor should be before the shortcut, and you will
learn what to expect once you select the shortcut.

Learn as many shortcuts as you can to become a true Excel 97
expert!

START AND EXIT

Start Excel . . . . `CLICK` ☒ Microsoft Excel
Find the Excel program on the Windows Start menu.
*To do so, press **Ctrl Esc**, and select **Programs**,*
Microsoft Excel.

Go to next program . . . . Alt Esc

Cycle through programs . . . . Alt Tab
*Hold down **Alt** and press **Tab** repeatedly until the*
open program that you want to use appears.

Maximize window size . . . . `2CLICK` title bar
Repeat to restore to original size.

Exit Excel . . . . Alt F4 *or* ☒

MENUS

Access menu . . . . / or **Alt** or **F10**

Shortcut menu . . . . **Shift F10** or ` RCLICK `

Document menu . . . . **Alt -**

Application menu . . . . **Alt Spacebar**

Windows' Start menu . . . . **Ctrl Esc**

Cancel command . . . . **Esc** or **Alt** or **F10**

Access toolbar from keyboard . . . . **Alt, Ctrl Tab**
*Press and release **Alt**, then press **Ctrl Tab** repeatedly
to select toolbar. Press arrow keys to select a tool,
and press **Enter**.*

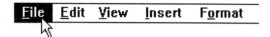

OPEN AND CREATE WORKBOOKS

Open workbook (*.xls)
or template (*.xlt) . . . . Ctrl O *or*

Create workbook from template . . . . Alt FN

Create new blank workbook . . . . Ctrl N *or*

PREVIEW

Preview . . . .

Zoom (in/out) . . . . **CLICK**

Move around . . . . ↑ ↓ ← → PgUp PgDn

First page . . . . Ctrl ↑ *or* ←

Last page . . . . Ctrl ↓ *or* →

Exit preview . . . . Esc

PRINT

Set up page . . . . Alt FU
*Set margins, footers, page size, orientation, gridlines,
etc.*

Print (displays dialog box) . . . . Ctrl P
*First, hold down **Ctrl** and click tabs of sheets to print
to print only selected sheets if desired.*

Print automatically. . . . .

SAVE AND CLOSE WORKBOOK

<u>S</u>ave . . . . Ctrl S *or*

Save and name or convert. F12

<u>C</u>lose. . . . . Ctrl F4 *or* ⊠

<u>C</u>lose all workbooks. . . . . Alt Shift F, C

Close all and <u>e</u>xit . . . . Alt F4 *or* ⊠

WORKSPACE FILES

Workspace remembers which document windows are open.

Save windows to a <u>w</u>orkspace file . . . . Alt FW

<u>O</u>pen workspace (*.xlw) . . . . Ctrl O *or*

| File | **Edit** | View | Insert | Format |

UNDO AND REPEAT

Undo . . . . **Ctrl Z** *or* ↺ ▾
Undoes the last command or format. Not available
for all commands.

Redo . . . . ↻ ▾
This undoes the previous Undo command.

Repeat **F4**
Repeats the last command or format. Not available
for all commands.

MOVE IN A WORKBOOK

Cell A1	**Ctrl Home**
End of active area	**Ctrl End**
End of block of cells	**Ctrl ↑ ↓ ← →**
Screen left/right	**Alt PgUp/Alt PgDn**
Scroll to display active cell	**Ctrl Backspace**
Go to cell or range	**F5** *or* range_name ▾
Previous sheet	**Ctrl PgUp**
Next sheet	**Ctrl PgDn**

SCROLL SHEET TABS

Scroll tabs left/right . . . . ▤ / ▤

Beginning/end of tabs . . . . ◀ / ▶

View more tabs . . . . DRAG ▣   She⬌

View default number of tabs . . . . 2CLICK ▣   She⬌

Rename a tab . . . . 2CLICK ▣   \Sheet/

FORMULA OPERATORS

Numeric formulas . . . . + - * / ^ %

String (text) formulas . . . . &

Logical formulas . . . . < > = <= >= <>

Logical functions . . . . AND(x,y) OR(x,y) NOT(x)

SAMPLE FORMULAS

=5*B2
Formula with a relative cell address.

=5*B2
Formula with an absolute cell address.

=1.2*PRICE
A formula can refer to a named range.

=West Sales
Formula can refer to the intersection of row and column labels.

=SUM(G9:G11)
Formula with a function. A colon indicates a range.

{=B2:B9*.01}
An array fills as many cells as there are results. First select cells to contain results, type formula, and press **Ctrl Shift Enter**.

{={1,2,3;4,5,6}*{.3}}
Do not type {} manually in arrays except around constants. Separate constants in a row with a comma. Separate rows in array with a semicolon.

{=SUM(B2:D2*B3:D3)}
Some arrays create only one result in one cell.

=SUM([BUDGET.XLS]Nov:Dec!C1:D9)
A formula can refer to data in another workbook.

=[http://www.invest.com/quotes.xls]Sheet1!A2
Filename can be http (World Wide Web) address.

=[ftp://ftp.invest.com/pub/quotes.xls]Sheet1!A2
Filename can be ftp (File Transfer Protocol) address.

EDIT IN THE FORMULA BAR

| range_name ▼ | X ✓ = | Chief Executive Officer |

Edit a cell . . . . F2 *or* `2CLICK` cell

Insert/overtype . . . . **Ins**

Insert range name. . . . . F3 *or* `range_name ▼`

Insert function name. . . . . Shift F3 *or* `fx`

Insert function arguments using
Function Wizard . . . . Ctrl A *or* `=`
First type the function name.

Insert function arguments. . . . . Ctrl Shift A
First type the function name.

Point to cell . . . . `CLICK` cell *or* `DRAG` range
Or, `CLICK` *first cell in range and use cell selection
keys. See* **Select Cells** *below.*

Absolute/relative/mixed reference F4

Select word or cell address . . . . `2CLICK`

Select any text. . . . . `DRAG`

Delete character right/left. . . . . Del/Backspace

Delete to end of line . . . . Ctrl Del

Insert a new line. . . . . Alt Enter

Convert formula to value F9

Copy formula from cell above . . . . Ctrl '

Copy value from cell above . . . . Ctrl Shift "

Sum cells above (or to the left) . . . . Alt = *or* $\boxed{\Sigma}$
*In Edit mode, press **Alt =** twice.*

FINISH EDITING IN FORMULA BAR

Cancel changes . . . . Esc *or* $\boxed{\times}$

Enter formula (save changes) . . . . Enter *or* $\boxed{\checkmark}$

Enter and move up in range . . . . Shift Enter

Enter formula and move to next cell . . . . Tab

Enter formula in selected cells . . . . Ctrl Enter
*Select cells, type formula, then **Ctrl Enter**.*

Enter formula as an array . . . . Ctrl Shift Enter
*See **Sample Formulas** above.*

DATE AND TIME

Current date (does not update) . . . . Ctrl ;

Current time (does not update) . . . . Ctrl Shift :

Current date (updates) . . . . =TODAY()

Current date and time (updates) . . . . =NOW()

Convert number to date . . . . Ctrl Shift #

Convert number to time . . . . Ctrl Shift @

GROUP SHEETS

Grouping sheets is different from selecting cells. Group sheets before issuing a command to affect several sheets at once. You can insert or delete cells/rows/columns, select cells, format, or type on all sheets of the group at once.

Group range of sheets . . . . **CLICK** first tab,
Shift **CLICK** last tab

Group non-adjacent sheets. . . . . **Ctrl CLICK** tabs

Group all sheets . . . . **RCLICK** tab, **S**

Select all cells in grouped sheets . . . . **Ctrl A**
Selecting one or more cells affects all corresponding cells in the group.

Ungroup sheets . . . . **RCLICK** tab, **U**

SELECT CELLS

*To select based on cell data, see **Select Special** below. See also **Move Between Selected Cells** below.*

Cell range . . . . **DRAG** *or* Shift $\uparrow \downarrow \leftarrow \rightarrow$ *or* **F8** $\rightarrow$

3D range . . . . **Ctrl CLICK** sheet tabs,
then select cells on one of the sheets

Column . . . . **Ctrl Spacebar** *or* **CLICK** column letter
For multiple columns, **DRAG** *column headings.*

Row. . . . . **Shift Spacebar** *or* **CLICK** row number
For multiple rows, **DRAG** *row headings.*

Entire sheet .... Ctrl Shift Spacebar *or* Ctrl A
or CLICK ☐ *(above row numbers)*

All active cells in sheet .... Ctrl Home,
Shift Ctrl End

To first cell in row .... Shift Home

To last cell in row .... End, Shift Enter

To next non-blank cell
(any direction) .... Shift Ctrl ↑ ↓ ← →

Cell nonadjacent to selection .... Ctrl CLICK ☐

Range nonadjacent to selection .... Ctrl DRAG ☐

Multiple ranges on/off .... Shift F8
*After you press **Shift F8**, use any method to select*
*more cell ranges. No need to **Ctrl** DRAG ☐ to select*
the next range; just DRAG ☐.

Scroll to display active cell .... Ctrl Backspace

Reduce or expand selection .... Shift ↑ ↓ ← →

Unselect .... Shift Backspace
Returns to the active cell.

MOVE BETWEEN SELECTED CELLS

Move right .... Tab

Move left .... Shift Tab

Move down .... Enter

Move up .... Shift Enter

Next corner of selection . . . . **Ctrl .** *(period)*

Next nonadjacent selection . . . . **Ctrl Alt →**

Previous nonadjacent selection . . . . **Ctrl Alt ←**

SELECT SPECIAL

Handy for troubleshooting formulas.

View auditing toolbar on/off . . . . **Alt TUS**

Select current array . . . . **Ctrl /**

Select current region . . . . **Ctrl Shift ***
Selects up to next blank cell in all directions.

Select direct dependents . . . . **Ctrl]**

Select all dependents . . . . **Ctrl Shift]**

Select direct precedents . . . . **Ctrl [**

Select all precedents . . . . **Ctrl Shift [**

Select all cells with comments . . . . **Ctrl Shift O**

**Select comments, constants,
formulas** . . . . **Ctrl G, Alt S**

Select different content in row . . . . **Ctrl **
*First, select rows to search. Finds cells that do not
match cell in column marked by active cell.*

Select different content in column. . . . . **Ctrl Shift |**
First, select columns to search. Finds cells that do not
match cell in row marked by active cell.

Select visible (non-hidden) cells only . . . . **Alt ;**

MOVE CELL DATA

First, select cells with data to move.

Cut to Clipboard . . . . **Ctrl X** *or* ✂️

Paste from Clipboard. . . . . **Enter** *or* **Ctrl V** *or* 📋
First, position cell pointer in top left corner of range
to contain moved data.

Move with mouse . . . . **DRAG** border
First, point to border of selected cells until pointer
changes to an arrow. To move sheet, **DRAG** *sheet*
tab.

Move and insert . . . . **Shift DRAG** border
First, point to border of selected cells until pointer
changes to an arrow.

Move and insert (menu) . . . . **RDRAG** border

Shortcut menu . . . . **Shift F10** *or* **RCLICK**

COPY CELL DATA

First, select cells with data to copy.

Copy to Clipboard . . . . **Ctrl C** *or* 📑

Paste and link to file or Web page. . . . . **Alt ES Alt L**

Paste from Clipboard. . . . . **Enter** *or* **Ctrl V** *or* 🖌

First, position cell pointer in top left corner of range
to contain copied data, or select a range of cells.

Copy with mouse . . . . **Ctrl** `DRAG` border
To copy an entire sheet, ***Ctrl*** `DRAG` *tab.*

Copy and insert . . . . **Ctrl Shift** `DRAG` border

Copy and insert (menu) . . . . `RDRAG` border

Copy formula from cell above . . . . **Ctrl '**

Copy value from cell above . . . . **Ctrl Shift "**

CLEAR CELL DATA OR FORMAT

Clear contents of selected cell(s) . . . . **Del**
Leaves formatting in cell.

Clear contents, comments, and format. . . . . **Alt EAA**

Clear format only . . . . **Alt EAF**

Clear contents (mouse) . . . . `DRAG` handle (+) up
Handle is found in lower right corner of selection.

DELETE CELLS

The following procedures shift cells, rows, column, or sheets to
close up the gap created by deletions.

Delete cell range, rows, or columns . . . . **Ctrl -**
First, select the cells, columns, or rows to delete.

Delete with mouse. . . . . **Shift** `DRAG` handle (+) up
First, select the cells, columns, or rows to delete.
Handle is found in lower right corner of selection.

Delete current sheet. . . . . **Alt EL** *or* `RCLICK` tab, **D**

FILL SELECTED CELLS

First, select cells. Contents of first cell in selection are repeated to other cells in the selection.

Fill right . . . . **Ctrl R**

Fill down . . . . **Ctrl D**

Fill with mouse. . . . . **Ctrl** `DRAG` handle (+)
Handle is found in lower right corner of selection.

Fill with series . . . . **value(s),** `DRAG` handle (+)
First, type one or two starting values for the data
series (e.g., Jan or 5,10), then `DRAG` *cells to fill.*

FIND AND REPLACE CELL DATA

Find a formula, value, or comment . . . . **Ctrl F**

Find next . . . . **Shift F4**

Find previous . . . . **Ctrl Shift F4**

Replace a formula, value, or comment. . . . . **Ctrl H**

ZOOM

Zoom (dialog box)	`RCLICK` title bar
Zoom	`75%` ▼

DISPLAY OPTIONS

Preview and adjust page breaks	Alt VP
Display objects (on/off/placeholders)	Ctrl 6
Display formulas or values (toggle)	Ctrl `
Display outline symbols (on/off)	Ctrl 8

TOOLBARS

Show/hide Standard toolbar	Ctrl 7
Hide all toolbars.	Alt VU
Open/close a toolbar	`RCLICK` a toolbar
Show at top of screen.	`2CLICK` title bar
Show in a palette	`DRAG` left edge
Move toolbar.	`DRAG` title bar
Change shape of toolbar.	`DRAG` border

INSERT CELLS

Insert cell range, rows, columns . . . . **Ctrl Shift +**
*First, select as many cells, columns, or rows as you
would like to insert. New cells, rows, or columns are
inserted before selection.*

Insert with mouse . . . . **Shift** DRAG handle (+)
*First, select as many cells, columns, or rows as you
would like to insert. Handle is found in lower right
corner of selection.*

Insert new sheet (before current) . . . . **Shift F11**

Insert new chart sheet **F11**

Insert new Excel 4.0 macro sheet . . . . **Ctrl F11**

RANGE NAMES

Name cell range . . . . **Ctrl F3** *or* `range_name ▼`

Name from cell data . . . . **Ctrl Shift F3**
*Creates names from top row or left column of
selection.*

Go to a named range . . . . **F5** *or* `range_name ▼`

List range names . . . . **F3** *or* `range_name ▼`

CELL COMMENTS

Add comment to current cell . . . . Shift F2
A red box appears in the upper right corner of cell.

Insert line break in comment . . . . Enter

Edit comment . . . . Shift F2

View all comments (toolbar) . . . . Alt VC

Display comment permanently . . . . ▢ RCLICK , O

Find a comment . . . . Shift F5

Delete a comment . . . . Alt EAM

Select all cells with comments . . . . Ctrl Shift O

Move to next selected comment . . . . Tab

Move to previous selected comment . . . . Shift Tab

Set display options . . . . Alt TO, View tab

Print comments . . . . Alt FU, Sheet tab

HYPERLINKS

A hyperlink makes a cell or graphic into an active object. If the user clicks on a hyperlink, the designated document (on a local hard drive, server, or Internet site) will open. You can also use hyperlinks to create and pre-address an e-mail message (e.g., mailto:hparks@microref.com).

Hyperlink selected cell or graphic . . . . Ctrl K
Example: http://www.microref.com.

Activate hyperlink . . . . `CLICK`

Select cell without activating
hyperlink . . . . arrow keys

Select graphic without
activating hyperlink . . . . Ctrl `CLICK`

Change text of hyperlink . . . . type over cell

Change hyperlink . . . . `RCLICK` H

Format   **Tools**   **Data**   **Window**

FONT AND ALIGNMENT

Format selected cells or selected text within a cell.

Format cells or text . . . . Ctrl 1

Change font . . . . Helvetica ▾

Change size . . . . Ctrl 1 *or* 10 ▾

Bold (on/off) . . . . Ctrl B *or* **B**

Italic (on/off) . . . . Ctrl I *or* *I*

Underline (on/off) . . . . Ctrl U *or* U̲

Strikeout text (on/off) . . . . Ctrl 5

Align text within cells . . . . ≡ *or* ≡ *or* ≡

Center cell across selected columns . . . . ↔a↔

Apply or create a style . . . . Alt '

Shortcut menu . . . . Shift F10 *or* ☐ RCLICK

FORMAT NUMBERS

General numeric format . . . . Ctrl Shift ~

$13,000.00 . . . . Ctrl Shift $ *or* $

12% . . . . Ctrl Shift % or %

13,000.00 . . . . Ctrl Shift ! or ,

Increase displayed decimals . . . . +.0 .00

Decrease displayed decimals . . . . .00 +.0

3.98E+44 . . . . Ctrl Shift ^

12-Jan-98 . . . . Ctrl Shift #

2:30 PM . . . . Ctrl Shift @

Format cells (dialog box) . . . . Ctrl 1

Shortcut menu . . . . Shift F10 or ▮RCLICK

COPY FORMATS

Copy formats of selected cell . . . . 🖌
Then, DRAG▯ cells to format.

ROW HEIGHT AND COLUMN WIDTH

<u>R</u>ow height . . . . DRAG▯ border below heading

<u>R</u>ow best fit . . . . 2CLICK▯ border below heading

Hide <u>r</u>ows . . . . Ctrl 9

Show hidden <u>r</u>ows . . . . Ctrl Shift 9
First, select rows surrounding hidden rows.

<u>C</u>olumn width . . . . DRAG▯ border right of heading

Column best fit .... `2CLICK` border right of heading
Sets the width to fit the longest data in the column.

Hide columns .... **Ctrl 0** *(zero)*

Show hidden columns .... **Ctrl Shift 0** *(zero)*
First, select columns surrounding hidden columns.

BORDERS AND COLORS

Border cell(s) .... **Ctrl Shift &** *or* ⊞▾

Remove borders .... **Ctrl Shift _** *(underscore)*

Cell color .... 🎨▾

Text color .... 🅰▾

| **Tools** | **Data** | **Window** | **Help** |

SPELLING

Check spelling . . . . F7 *or* ✅

SET DEFAULTS

Change defaults . . . . Alt TO

Display objects (on/off/placeholders) . . . . Ctrl 6

Show/hide Standard toolbar . . . . Ctrl 7

Toggle display of formulas or values . . . . Ctrl `

CALCULATE FORMULAS

Set calculation to manual . . . . Alt TO

Calculate current sheet . . . . Shift F9

Calculate all open workbooks . . . . Ctrl = *or* F9

DATABASE (LIST)

To create a database, set up a list with field names in the top row of each column. Type each record in a separate row.

<u>S</u>ort records . . . . Alt DS *or* ![A-Z sort] *or* ![Z-A sort]

Auto<u>F</u>ilter (on/off) . . . . **Alt DFF**

Set va<u>l</u>id entries . . . . **Alt DL**

Create a <u>p</u>ivot table . . . . **Alt DP**

Sub<u>t</u>otal . . . . **Alt DB**

<u>G</u>roup and outline automatically . . . . **Alt DGA**

EDIT RECORDS WITH A FORM

Use a f<u>o</u>rm. . . . . **Alt DO**

Go to previous/next field . . . . **Shift Tab/Tab**

Go to previous/next record . . . . ↑↓

Create a new record . . . . **Ctrl PgDn**

Find records with criteria. . . . . **Alt C**
*Use * and ? wildcards. Examples: S* Sm?th Use < > =*
<= >= <>. Examples: <5000   >m.

OUTLINE

Outlined Sheet

	A	B	C	D	E
1		Jan-94	Feb-94	Mar-94	1st Q
3	Total Salaries	$ 46,958	$ 27,300	$ 22,169	$ 96,427
5	Total Office Supplies	$ 7,308	$ 6,899	$ 9,015	$ 23,222
7	Total Travel	$ 10,223	$ 5,420	$ 3,513	$ 19,156
8	Rent	$ 22,000	$ 22,000	$ 22,000	$ 66,000
9	TOTAL EXPENSES	$ 86,489	$ 61,619	$ 56,697	$204,805

Create outline from selected cells . . . . **Alt DGA**

Promote to higher level . . . . **Alt Shift ←**
First, select row(s) or column(s) to promote.

Demote to lower level . . . . **Alt Shift →**
First, select row(s) or column(s) to demote.

Show/hide outline symbols . . . . **Ctrl 8**

Collapse heading . . . . [−]
Collapses levels under the heading to hide detail.
Collapse levels to view or print a summary report.

Expand heading . . . . [+]
Expands a collapsed heading to show lower levels.

Select heading and detail . . . . **Shift CLICK** [−]
Selects a heading and all levels under it.

Remove outline. . . . . **Alt DGC**

| **Tools** | **Data** | **Window** | **Help** |

DOCUMENT WINDOWS

A workbook appears in a document window. To see different sheets at the same time or different parts of the same sheet, open multiple windows for a single workbook.

Open new window on current
workbook . . . . Alt WN *or* `RCLICK` title bar

Arrange all . . . . Alt WA *or* `RCLICK` title bar

Previous window . . . . Ctrl Tab *or* Ctrl F6

Next window. . . . . Ctrl Shift Tab *or* Ctrl Shift F6

Close window . . . . Ctrl F4

SPLIT WINDOW INTO PANES

Split bars (▯ and ▭) are located on the scroll bars.

Split into panes . . . . `DRAG` ▯ *or* ▭

Split into four panes at cell pointer . . . . Alt WS

Freeze top and/or left panes (on/off) . . . . Alt WF

Next pane F6

Remove split . . . . `2CLICK` split bar

Excel Interprets What You Type

You can type data into any cell. As you type, Excel interprets the characters to see if you are typing text, a number, or a formula.

Numbers Take Many Forms

You can add a dollar sign, commas, decimal point, or percent sign to a number as you type. Excel applies a numeric format. The format does not change the actual underlying value.

Dates are Numbers, Too

If you type a date or time into a cell, Excel stores it as a number. For example: 1/1/97 12:00 PM is stored as 35431.5. Perform date mathematics, such as adding 30 to a "Date Issued" date.

All Formulas are Created with Equal

When typing a formula into a cell, type an = sign first to indicate to Excel that it is not text. Excel will calculate the results.

Excel's Built-In Functions

One of Excel's key strengths lies in its ability to perform complex operations. Whether you are a statistician, engineer, or business person, Excel's **Shift F3** functions provide the tools for your job.

Sheet Names Create Order

The bottom of the screen indicates how cells are stored on individual sheets, like pages in a book. Double-click a sheet tab to rename it something like August or 1999 or North.

Group Sheets to Look Alike

If you need to format or edit several sheets at one time, you can "group" (and "ungroup") sheets by holding down **Ctrl** and clicking on their names.

Group sheets before you insert or delete columns or rows, select cells, format, or type. The change is applied to all sheets in the group.

Identify Cells by the Intersection

...of its sheet, column, and row. For example: Summary!F4 is column F, row 4 in a sheet named Summary. Excel assumes that you are referring to the current sheet unless you specify otherwise.

You Can Refer to Several Cells

In a command or formula, to refer to adjacent cells, use the format F4:G6 or North:West!F4:G6. Or, drag the mouse over the cells to select.

Templates Unify Workbooks

Templates are model workbooks or sheets that Excel copies to the screen every time you create a workbook or insert a sheet. Create templates by saving formatted workbooks with a .XLT file type. Several templates are included on the Spreadsheet Solutions tab in the New dialog box (**File, New**).

Charts Analyze and Present

Charts are either embedded in a worksheet or placed on a separate sheet before the data upon which it is based. Or cut and paste charts in other files.

Excel Manipulates Lists

Excel's Data command helps you manipulate and analyze data from external databases and Excel lists. Use **Data, Get External Data** to import into Excel.

QUICK LIST OF SHORTCUTS

Open Workbook

Open workbook, workspace or template . . . . Ctrl O
Create blank workbook. . . . . Ctrl N
Create workbook from template. . . . . Alt FN
Open previously open workbook. . . . . Alt *num.*
View numbered files at bottom of the menu.

Print Workbook

Set up page. . . . . Alt FU
Set margins, page size, orientation, gridlines, etc.
Insert/remove a page break. . . . . Alt IB
Preview *(Esc to exit)* . . . . 🔍
Print using dialog box . . . . Ctrl P
Print using defaults. . . . . 🖨

Close Workbook

Save. . . . . Ctrl S
Save and name or convert F12
Save windows to workspace file . . . . Alt FW
Remembers open files and window arrangement.
Close workbook. . . . . Ctrl F4
Close all workbooks . . . . Alt Shift F, C
Close all and exit Excel . . . . Alt F4

Edit in Formula Bar

Edit a cell. . . . . F2 *or* `2 CLICK` cell
Start a formula . . . . =
Examples: =5*B2   =SUM(G9:G11)   {=B2:B9*.01}
Insert/overtype. . . . . Ins
Insert range name. F3
Insert function name *(Wizard)*. . . . . Shift F3
Insert function arguments *(Wizard)* . . . . Ctrl A
Insert function arguments . . . . Ctrl Shift A
Insert a new line . . . . Alt Enter
Select any text. . . . . `DRAG`

Delete to end of line . . . . Ctrl Del
Change reference *(absolute/relative/mixed)* F4
Convert formula to value. F9
Sum cells above or to the left . . . . Alt =
In Edit mode, press Alt = twice.

Insert Date or Time

Current date *(does not update)* . . . . Ctrl ;
Current time *(does not update)* . . . . Ctrl Shift :
Current date *(updates)* . . . . =TODAY()
Current date and time *(updates)* . . . . =NOW()
Convert number to date. . . . . Ctrl Shift #
Convert number to time . . . . Ctrl Shift @

Experts' Pick

AutoFormat table . . . . Alt OA
Best fit row/column . . . . 2 CLICK border
Delete row or column . . . . Ctrl -
Format cell or text . . . . Ctrl 1
Go to end of block . . . . 2 CLICK cell border
Go to previous/next sheet . . . . Ctrl PgUp/PgDn
Insert date. . . . . Ctrl ;
Insert function *(Wizard)* . . . . Shift F3
Insert hyperlink . . . . Ctrl K
Insert row or column . . . . Ctrl +
Select entire sheet. . . . . Ctrl A
Shortcut menu. Shift F10 or RCLICK
Sum cells above *(or to left)* . . . . Alt =

Sample Formulas

Relative cell address. . . . . =5*B2
Absolute cell address . . . . =5*B2
Range name. . . . . =1.2*PRICE
Function and range . . . . =SUM(G9:G11)
External . . . . =SUM([YEAR.XLS]Nov:Dec!C1:D9)
One-cell array . . . . {=SUM(B2:D2*B3:D3)}
Type formula (no {}) and Ctrl Shift Enter.

	F1	F2	F3	F4
C+S			Create Name	
C			Define Name	Close Document
A	New Chart Sheet	Save As		Exit Excel
S	What Is?	Insert Comment	Function Wizard	Repeat Find/Go To
U	Help	Edit Mode	Paste Name	Repeat/Absolute

	F1	F2	F3	F4
C+S		Previous Window		
C	Restore Window	Next Window	Move Window	Size Window
A				Macro Dialog Box
S	Find	Previous Pane		Add to Selection
U	Go To	Next Pane	Spelling	Extend Mode

	F1	F2	F3	F4
C+S				Print
C	Minimize Window	Maximize Window	4.0 Macro Sheet	Open
A			Visual Basic Editor	
S	Calc. Active Sheet	Shortcut Menu	New Sheet	Save
U	Calc. Workbooks	Menu	New Chart Sheet	Save As

C+S = CTRL + SHIFT   C = CTRL   A = ALT   S = SHIFT   U = UNSHIFT